SLIMMING SOUP RECIPES UNDER
100, 200, 300 & 400
CALORIES

Slimming
SOUP
MAKER
recipe book

Sophia Hobbs

INTRODUCTION 5

Slimming VEGETABLE SOUPS

CONTENTS

Slimming MEAT & SEAFOOD SOUPS

Great British soups but *slimmer*! A new collection of delicious calorie-counted soup recipes for soup maker machines...with no need to sauté!

Homemade, tasty soup recipes for the calorie-conscious and anyone on a slimming journey, a low-carb, low-cholesterol or weight-loss diet. Using some smart ingredient swaps, everyone can create a comfort-loving bowl of soup with fewer calories from my new cookbook of slimming recipes.

Influenced by my popular, tried and tested Soup Maker Recipe Books, but with new additions, adaptions, ideas and inspiration for guilt-free, healthy and hearty recipes.

My Soup Maker & Recipes

Choosing Your Ingredients

Each recipe in this soup book has been written and tested in the UK, using everyday ingredients available in all UK supermarkets and written in UK measurements. There are no exotic, fancy or unique recipes – just really tasty, everyday soups. Plus, you don't have to sauté ingredients prior to making these recipes in your soup maker machine. So, with or without a sauté function on your device, these are the perfect recipes for you and your soup maker!

You'll notice sometimes I opt for tinned or ready-made ingredients, like pre-cooked rice or tinned tomatoes rather than fresh tomatoes; this is to keep things simple and fuss-free. If you have plenty of time on your hands, feel free to make things from scratch or substitute in fresh versions if you wish.

Also, sometimes I'll mention fresh herbs rather than dried herbs and vice versa. Don't let any of this stop you if you don't have the exact ingredients to hand. Dried herbs can usually be substituted for fresh herbs and vice versa, just be careful not to overdo it as dried herbs generally have a more concentrated flavour. You'll notice garlic features in many of the soup recipes included in this book. Garlic is widely used as it imparts a distinctive taste and depth to the soup; if, however, you are not a fan of garlic, consider reducing the amount in the recipe or experiment with other herbs and spices to suit your taste.

I have tried to keep all the ingredients simple and easy to work with. For example, rather than saying 200g of potatoes, I have listed it as a medium potato. If your potato is 180g or 220g it really doesn't matter, it's just a general guide to a rough weight measurement. To follow is a list of the average weights of many of the ingredients I use:

1 butternut squash 500g	**1 leek 200g**	**1 medium carrot 150g**
1 pumpkin 500g	**1 broccoli head 350g**	**1 cauliflower head 600g**
1 medium potato 200g	**1 courgette 200g**	**1 swede 600g**
1 medium sweet potato 300g	**1 medium parsnip 180g**	
1 medium onion 180g	**1 aubergine 250g**	

Using Your Soup Maker

I used a Morphy Richards 1.6 Litre Soup Maker to test our recipes. This makes approx. 4 servings (more if you're using mugs). You may have a different machine but don't worry, that's OK. You can still use the recipes but may need to make some minor adjustments, such as reducing quantities of ingredients if you have a smaller capacity soup maker. If your device does not use pre-programmed cooking settings then you should follow the manufacturer's instructions regarding cooking times. As a guide, a Morphy Richards 1.6L machine cooks for 21 minutes for a smooth soup and 28 minutes for chunky.

Some soup makers have the option to sauté ingredients. All my recipes are written with no requirement to sauté any ingredient prior to cooking, so if your machine does not have a sauté function then these are the perfect recipes for you and your soup maker.

Sautéing does, however, have its place when making some soups, intensifying the flavours of some ingredients to make a richer, more flavoursome soup. So, for those who want to take the time to sauté some ingredients on the stove prior to adding to the soup maker, go ahead and sauté any onions, garlic, leeks and celery in a little olive oil for a few minutes first. If, however, a one-pot, cook-and-go soup is what you're looking for, I've got you covered!

Please note that only pre-cooked meats and fish can be used in your soup maker. Do not use raw meat or fish ingredients.

Perhaps the most important factor to adhere to when using your soup maker is never to go past the maximum fill line indicated on the machine jug or go below the minimum. These guides are there for a reason and will prevent the danger of the soup maker's hot ingredients spilling out, or the heating element burning out due to insufficient liquid. The Morphy Richards machine is equipped with an automatic cut off which prevents the blade from turning should the max line be exceeded. For this reason, each recipe advises stock quantity within a range e.g. 600-800ml and as one of the final ingredients to be added to your soup maker (before any pre-cooked items or garnish). This will allow for differing weights and sizes of other ingredients e.g. a medium potato and will ensure you don't exceed the maximum fill line. It also allows you to have a little control over the consistency of your soup.

I have indicated the consistency mode (smooth/chunky) for each recipe; however, this is a personal preference. If you prefer a smooth consistency where chunky is stated, just choose the appropriate setting on your soup maker or select the blend mode at the end of cooking to alter the final consistency. That's the beauty of how versatile soup and your soup maker can be! The chunky mode on Morphy Richards soup makers (and most other manufacturers) allows the ingredients to be heated for longer to ensure the chunky ingredients are fully cooked. For chunky soup there is no blending process, just heating; it is therefore best to cut any vegetables into small dice-sized pieces. If your soup is a little too chunky after cooking, select the blend function to achieve the desired consistency.

Some soup maker models have a pause function to allow you to remove the lid and add ingredients which may require less cooking time than set by the pre-programed modes or to allow you to check seasoning. If your soup maker doesn't have this functionality don't worry, you can add any extras at the end and warm through.

Some soup makers also have a 'clean' function to help with any stubborn ingredients that may have stuck to the heating plate of your device. This option can be handy for cleaning, however filling the jug of the machine to soak in a little hot water with washing up liquid will do just as well. Do not immerse the whole machine in water. You will find that unfortunately on occasion some ingredients will catch and burn on the heating plate and sometimes this can cause the program to stop. Making sure the ingredients are not too large and stirring the contents can help prevent this.

Please make sure you read all the manufacturer's instructions and guidelines before using your soup maker. Because soup makers are relatively simple machines, the instructions are not lengthy and will give you some helpful tips to get the best from your device.

Stock/Beware of Salt

Stock is an essential base for a great tasting soup. There are two options:
- Shop-bought stock. Either cubes/bouillon powder or fresh stock in the chilled section of a supermarket
- Homemade stock

Either will make a great soup and obviously a shop-bought option is far easier and works in perfect tandem with the fuss-free nature of making soup in a soup machine. Homemade stock, however, is preferred by some and can add an extra depth of taste to your soup. I've included 4 basic and easy stock recipes at the end of this book that you could try. They can all be made in batches and frozen for easy use when you need them.

A word of warning when using shop-bought stock or bouillon powder is to check the levels of salt. Often overuse of salt can be the main cause of a ruined soup, particularly if you also add additional seasoning, not to mention the negative health consequences of consuming more than the maximum daily recommended salt intake (6mg per day for adults). Try to check the ingredient list of stock cubes and powders and opt for ones that contain reduced levels. Look out for brands that have started selling 'zero salt' stock cubes.

If in doubt, opt for a less concentred mix of stock cube to water when making your soup. Remember that additional seasoning can be added at the end of the cooking process if needed.

I hope you enjoy this new collection of great British *slimming* soups and have fun with your soup maker.

CARROT & ORANGE SOUP

SERVES 4
smooth

Calories: 81 | **Protein: 3g** | **Fat: 1g** | **Carbs: 19g** | **Fibre: 4g**

Ingredients

- 1 medium onion, chopped
- 4 medium carrots, chopped
- ½ tsp ground ginger
- 2 garlic cloves, sliced
- 600-800ml vegetable stock
- Zest & juice of 2 oranges
- 4 tbsp fresh flat leaf parsley, chopped
- Salt & pepper for seasoning

Method

ONE
Add all the ingredients, except the orange zest, juice, parsley and seasoning to your soup maker - making sure not to exceed the maximum fill line.

TWO
Combine all ingredients with a wooden spoon.

THREE
Secure the lid on the soup maker and select the smooth setting.

FOUR
When the soup is ready stir through the orange juice. Sprinkle with orange zest and parsley. Season and serve.

MUSHROOM & LENTIL SOUP

Calories: 109 | **Protein: 8g** | **Fat: 1g** | **Carbs: 20g** | **Fibre: 5g**

Ingredients

- 1 medium onion, chopped
- 1 celery stalk, sliced
- 1 tin (390g) cooked lentils, rinsed
- 100g mushrooms, sliced
- 1 tsp dried thyme
- 1 tsp dried rosemary
- 1 garlic clove, sliced
- 500-700ml vegetable stock
- 2 tbsp lemon juice
- Salt & pepper for seasoning

Method

ONE
Add all the ingredients, except the lemon juice and seasoning, to your soup maker - making sure not to exceed the maximum fill line.

TWO
Combine all ingredients with a wooden spoon.

THREE
Secure the lid on the soup maker and select the chunky setting.

FOUR
When the soup is ready stir through the lemon juice. Season and serve.

CAULIFLOWER CHEESE SOUP

SERVES 4
⬤ smooth

Calories: 220 | **Protein: 14g** | **Fat: 12g** | **Carbs: 17g** | **Fibre: 6g**

Ingredients

- 1 medium onion, chopped
- 1 medium carrot, chopped
- 1 cauliflower head, chopped
- 2 tsp Dijon mustard
- 1 garlic clove, sliced
- 600-800ml vegetable stock
- 120g Cheddar cheese, grated
- 4 tbsp fresh chives, chopped
- 2 tbsp toasted almond flakes, chopped (optional)
- Salt & pepper for seasoning

Method

ONE
Add all the ingredients, except the cheese, chives, almond flakes and seasoning, to your soup maker - making sure not to exceed the maximum fill line.

TWO
Combine all ingredients with a wooden spoon.

THREE
Secure the lid on the soup maker and select the smooth setting.

FOUR
When the soup is ready stir through the cheese until melted. Sprinkle with fresh chives and almonds. Season and serve.

CARROT & BEETROOT SOUP

SERVES 4
● smooth

Calories: 119	Protein: 4g	Fat: 1g	Carbs: 27g	Fibre: 5g

Ingredients

- 1 medium onion, chopped
- 2 medium carrots, chopped
- 2 cooked beetroots, chopped
- 1 tsp ground cumin
- ½ tsp ground coriander
- 1 garlic clove, sliced
- 500-700ml vegetable stock
- 1 raw beetroot, grated
- 4 tbsp fat free Greek yoghurt
- Salt & pepper for seasoning

Method

ONE
Add all the ingredients, except the raw beetroot, Greek yoghurt and seasoning to your soup maker - making sure not to exceed the maximum fill line.

TWO
Combine all ingredients with a wooden spoon.

THREE
Secure the lid on the soup maker and select the smooth setting.

FOUR
When the soup is ready, dollop the Greek yoghurt into the centre of each bowl and pile the grated beetroot over the top. Season and serve.

LEEK & TOMATO SOUP

7180

SERVES 4
● smooth

| Calories: 80 | Protein: 3g | Fat: 0g | Carbs: 19g | Fibre: 3g |

Ingredients

- 2 leeks, sliced
- 1 medium potato
- 2 garlic cloves, sliced
- 1 tin (400g) chopped tomatoes
- 1 tsp dried basil
- 1 tsp dried oregano
- 400ml-600ml vegetable stock
- Salt & pepper for seasoning

Method

ONE
Add all the ingredients to your soup maker - making sure not to exceed the maximum fill line.

TWO
Combine all ingredients with a wooden spoon.

THREE
Secure the lid on the soup maker and select the smooth setting.

FOUR
When the soup is ready season and serve.

LENTIL & SPINACH SOUP

SERVES 4
● smooth

| Calories: 111 | Protein: 8g | Fat: 1g | Carbs: 20g | Fibre: 6g |

Ingredients

- 1 medium onion, chopped
- 1 medium carrot, chopped
- 1 tin (390g) cooked lentils, rinsed
- 1 tsp dried thyme
- 2 garlic cloves, sliced
- 500-700ml vegetable stock
- 50g spinach
- Zest of 1 lemon
- Salt & pepper for seasoning

Method

ONE
Add all the ingredients, except the spinach, lemon zest and seasoning, to your soup maker - making sure not to exceed the maximum fill line.

TWO
Combine all ingredients with a wooden spoon. Once done, place the lid on the soup maker and select the smooth setting.

THREE
Five minutes before the end of the cooking time pause the cycle and add the spinach. If your soup maker doesn't have a pause function just add at the end, stir and warm through.

FOUR
When the soup is ready sprinkle with lemon zest, season and serve.

MEXICAN CORN SOUP

SERVES 4
smooth

Calories: 179 | **Protein: 7g** | **Fat: 8g** | **Carbs: 24g** | **Fibre: 8g**

Ingredients

- 1 medium onion, chopped
- 1 tin (390g) cooked lentils, rinsed
- ½ tin (200g) chopped tomatoes
- 100g frozen sweetcorn
- 1 tsp ground cumin
- 1 tsp paprika
- 1 garlic clove, sliced
- 400-600ml vegetable stock
- 1 medium ripe avocado, diced
- 2 tbsp lime juice
- Salt & pepper for seasoning

Method

ONE
Add all the ingredients, except the avocado, lime juice and seasoning, to your soup maker - making sure not to exceed the maximum fill line.

TWO
Combine all ingredients with a wooden spoon.

THREE
Secure the lid on the soup maker and select the smooth setting.

FOUR
When the soup is ready top with diced avocado and lime juice. Season and serve.

CARROT & CORIANDER SOUP

SERVES 4
● smooth

Calories: 91 | **Protein: 3g** | **Fat: 1g** | **Carbs: 20g** | **Fibre: 5g**

Ingredients

- 1 medium onion, chopped
- 1 medium potato, chopped
- 4 medium carrots, chopped
- 4 tbsp fresh coriander, chopped
- 1 garlic clove, sliced
- 600-800ml vegetable stock
- 4 spring onions, finely sliced
- Salt & pepper for seasoning

Method

ONE
Add all the ingredients, except the spring onions and seasoning, to your soup maker - making sure not to exceed the maximum fill line.

TWO
Combine all ingredients with a wooden spoon.

THREE
Secure the lid on the soup maker and select the smooth setting.

FOUR
When the soup is ready top with the sliced spring onions, season and serve.

LEEK & CAULIFLOWER SOUP

SERVES 4
● smooth

| Calories: 94 | Protein: 6g | Fat: 2g | Carbs: 15g | Fibre: 5g |

Ingredients

- 2 leeks, sliced
- 1 cauliflower head, chopped
- 2 garlic cloves, sliced
- 400ml-600ml vegetable stock
- 200ml semi-skimmed milk
- 4 tbsp fresh chives, chopped
- Salt & pepper for seasoning

Method

ONE
Add all the ingredients, except the milk, chives and seasoning, to your soup maker - making sure not to exceed the maximum fill line.

TWO
Combine all ingredients with a wooden spoon. Once done, place the lid on the soup maker and select the smooth setting.

THREE
Five minutes before the end of the cooking time pause the cycle and add the milk. If your soup maker doesn't have a pause function just add at the end, stir and warm through.

FOUR
When the soup is ready sprinkle with chopped chives, season and serve.

SPICED LENTIL SOUP

SERVES 4
●smooth

| Calories: 118 | Protein: 8g | Fat: 1g | Carbs: 21g | Fibre: 7g |

Ingredients

- 1 medium onion, chopped
- 1 medium carrot, chopped
- 1 tin (390g) cooked lentils, rinsed
- ½ tin (200g) chopped tomatoes
- 1 tsp ground coriander
- 1 tsp ground cumin
- ½ tsp cayenne pepper
- 1 garlic clove, sliced
- 300-500ml vegetable stock
- Salt & pepper for seasoning

Method

ONE
Add all the ingredients, except the seasoning to your soup maker - making sure not to exceed the maximum fill line.

TWO
Combine all ingredients with a wooden spoon.

THREE
Secure the lid on the soup maker and select the smooth setting.

FOUR
When the soup is ready, season and serve.

BROCCOLI CHEDDAR SOUP

SERVES 4
smooth

Calories: 158 | **Protein: 9g** | **Fat: 10g** | **Carbs: 11g** | **Fibre: 3g**

Ingredients

- 1 medium onion, chopped
- 1 broccoli head, chopped
- 1 tsp paprika
- 1 garlic clove, sliced
- 500-700ml vegetable stock
- 100ml semi-skimmed milk
- 100g Cheddar cheese, grated
- Salt & pepper for seasoning

Method

ONE
Add all the ingredients, except the milk, cheese and seasoning, to your soup maker - making sure not to exceed the maximum fill line.

TWO
Combine all ingredients with a wooden spoon. Once done, place the lid on the soup maker and select the smooth setting.

THREE
Three minutes before the end of the cooking time pause the cycle and add the milk. If your soup maker doesn't have a pause function just add at the end, stir and warm through.

FOUR
When the soup is ready, mound the grated cheese on top. Season and serve.

TUSCAN BEAN SOUP

SERVES 4
chunky

Calories: 119 | **Protein: 6g** | **Fat: 1g** | **Carbs: 23g** | **Fibre: 7g**

Ingredients

- 2 celery stalks, sliced
- 1 medium onion, chopped
- 1 medium carrot, chopped
- 1 tin (390g) white beans, rinsed
- 1 tsp dried thyme
- 1 tsp dried rosemary
- 1 garlic clove, sliced
- 500-700ml vegetable stock
- 2 tbsp balsamic vinegar
- Salt & pepper for seasoning

Method

ONE
Add all the ingredients, except the balsamic vinegar and seasoning to your soup maker - making sure not to exceed the maximum fill line.

TWO
Combine all ingredients with a wooden spoon.

THREE
Secure the lid on the soup maker and select the chunky setting.

FOUR
When the soup is ready, stir through the balsamic vinegar, season and serve.

SQUASH & RICE SOUP

SERVES 4
chunky

Calories: 120 | **Protein: 2g** | **Fat: 1g** | **Carbs: 26g** | **Fibre: 4g**

Ingredients

- 1 medium onion, chopped
- 1 medium carrot, chopped
- 1 medium butternut squash, chopped
- ½ pack (125g) pre-cooked white rice
- 1 tsp dried sage
- 1 tsp dried thyme
- 1 garlic clove, sliced
- 500-700ml vegetable stock
- 4 spring onions, finely sliced
- Salt & pepper for seasoning

Method

ONE
Add all the ingredients, except the spring onions and seasoning to your soup maker - making sure not to exceed the maximum fill line.

TWO
Combine all ingredients with a wooden spoon.

THREE
Secure the lid on the soup maker and select the chunky setting.

FOUR
When the soup is ready sprinkle with the spring onions, season and serve.

FILLING TOMATO SOUP

SERVES 4
👀 chunky

Calories: 106 | **Protein: 4g** | **Fat: 1g** | **Carbs: 22g** | **Fibre: 5g**

Ingredients

- 1 medium onion, chopped
- 2 celery stalks, sliced
- 1 medium carrot, chopped
- ½ pack (125g) pre-cooked quinoa
- 1 tin (400g) chopped tomatoes
- 1 tsp dried basil
- 1 garlic clove, sliced
- 500-700ml vegetable stock
- 8 ripe cherry tomatoes, finely chopped
- Salt & pepper for seasoning

Method

ONE
Add all the ingredients, except the fresh tomatoes and seasoning to your soup maker - making sure not to exceed the maximum fill line.

TWO
Combine all ingredients with a wooden spoon.

THREE
Secure the lid on the soup maker and select the chunky setting.

FOUR
When the soup is ready garnish with the fresh tomatoes. Season and serve.

SILKY LEEK & AVOCADO SOUP

SERVES 4
smooth

Calories: 185 | Protein: 4g | Fat: 12g | Carbs: 19g | Fibre: 6g

Ingredients

- 2 leeks, sliced
- 2 medium potatoes, chopped
- 2 garlic cloves, sliced
- 600ml-800ml vegetable stock
- 1 medium ripe avocado, diced
- 2 tbsp lime juice
- Salt & pepper for seasoning

Method

ONE
Add all the ingredients, except the avocado, lime juice and seasoning, to your soup maker - making sure not to exceed the maximum fill line.

TWO
Combine all ingredients with a wooden spoon.

THREE
Secure the lid on the soup maker and select the smooth setting.

FOUR
When the soup is ready top with diced avocado and lime juice. Season and serve.

CARROT & SWEET POTATO SOUP

7110

Calories: 119 | **Protein: 3g** | **Fat: 1g** | **Carbs: 28g** | **Fibre: 6g**

Ingredients

- 1 medium onion, chopped
- 3 medium carrots, chopped
- 1 medium sweet potato, chopped
- ½ tsp ground cinnamon
- 1 tsp ground cumin
- 2 garlic cloves, sliced
- 600-800ml vegetable stock
- 1 red pepper, very finely chopped
- Salt & pepper for seasoning

Method

ONE
Add all the ingredients, except the chopped pepper and seasoning, to your soup maker - making sure not to exceed the maximum fill line.

TWO
Combine all ingredients with a wooden spoon.

THREE
Secure the lid on the soup maker and select the smooth setting.

FOUR
When the soup is ready sprinkle over the finely chopped pepper, season and serve.

PARSNIP & APPLE SOUP

SERVES 4
● smooth

| Calories: 145 | Protein: 3g | Fat: 3g | Carbs: 29g | Fibre: 6g |

Ingredients

- 1 medium onion, chopped
- 2 medium parsnips, finely chopped
- 2 green apples, cored and chopped
- 1 tsp dried thyme
- ½ tsp ground nutmeg
- 1 garlic clove, sliced
- 500-700ml vegetable stock
- 100ml low-fat single cream
- Salt & pepper for seasoning

Method

ONE
Add all the ingredients, except the single cream and seasoning to your soup maker - making sure not to exceed the maximum fill line.

TWO
Combine all ingredients with a wooden spoon.

THREE
Secure the lid on the soup maker and select the smooth setting.

FOUR
When the soup is ready, stir through the cream, season and serve.

ROASTED PEPPER SOUP

Calories: 78 | **Protein: 2g** | **Fat: 1g** | **Carbs: 16g** | **Fibre: 4g**

Ingredients

- 1 medium onion, chopped
- ½ jar (200g) roasted red peppers
- 1 tin (400g) chopped tomatoes
- 1 garlic clove, sliced
- 1 tsp paprika
- 400-600ml vegetable stock
- 4 tbsp fresh basil, chopped
- Salt & pepper for seasoning

Method

ONE
Add all the ingredients, except the basil and seasoning, to your soup maker - making sure not to exceed the maximum fill line.

TWO
Combine all ingredients with a wooden spoon.

THREE
Secure the lid on the soup maker and select the smooth setting.

FOUR
When the soup is ready sprinkle with basil, season and serve.

CLASSIC ONION SOUP

SERVES 4
⚬ chunky

Calories: 174 | **Protein: 3g** | **Fat: 11g** | **Carbs: 20g** | **Fibre: 4g**

Ingredients

- 3 medium onions, chopped
- 4 garlic cloves, sliced
- 1 tsp dried thyme
- 2 tbsp low-fat 'butter' spread
- 600-800ml vegetable stock
- 2 tbsp extra virgin olive oil
- Salt & pepper for seasoning

Method

ONE
Add all the ingredients, except the olive oil and seasoning to your soup maker - making sure not to exceed the maximum fill line.

TWO
Combine all ingredients with a wooden spoon. Once done, place the lid on the soup maker and select the chunky setting.

THREE
Three minutes before the end of the cooking time pause the cycle and add the 'butter'. If your soup maker doesn't have a pause function just add at the end, stir and warm through.

FOUR
When the soup is ready, swirl in the olive oil. Season and serve with lots of black pepper.

SWEETCORN SOUP

SERVES 4
 chunky

Calories: 164 | **Protein: 5g** | **Fat: 5g** | **Carbs: 27g** | **Fibre: 4g**

Ingredients

- 1 medium onion, chopped
- 1 red pepper, chopped
- 400g frozen sweetcorn
- 1 tsp paprika
- 2 garlic cloves, sliced
- 500-700ml vegetable stock
- 100ml low-fat single cream
- 4 tbsp fresh chives, chopped
- Salt & pepper for seasoning

Method

ONE
Add all the ingredients, except the single cream, chives and seasoning to your soup maker - making sure not to exceed the maximum fill line.

TWO
Combine all ingredients with a wooden spoon.

THREE
Secure the lid on the soup maker and select the chunky setting.

FOUR
When the soup is ready stir through the cream. Sprinkle with chives, season and serve.

SPROUT & RADISH SOUP

SERVES 4
● smooth

Calories: 121 | **Protein: 5g** | **Fat: 8g** | **Carbs: 12g** | **Fibre: 6g**

Ingredients

- 1 medium onion, chopped
- 300g Brussels sprouts
- 2 garlic cloves, sliced
- 1 tsp ground cumin
- 500-700ml vegetable stock
- 100ml low-fat single cream
- 2 tbsp extra virgin olive oil
- 4 fresh radishes, finely chopped
- Salt & pepper for seasoning

Method

ONE
Add all the ingredients except the olive oil, radishes and seasoning to your soup maker - making sure not to exceed the maximum fill line.

TWO
Combine all ingredients with a wooden spoon.

THREE
Secure the lid on the soup maker and select the smooth setting.

FOUR
When the soup is ready drizzle with olive oil and pile the chopped radishes on top. Season and serve.

RED ONION & BALSAMIC SOUP

SERVES 4
😀 chunky

Calories: 137 | **Protein: 2g** | **Fat: 7g** | **Carbs: 19g** | **Fibre: 3g**

Ingredients

- 3 medium red onions, chopped
- 2 garlic cloves, sliced
- 2 tbsp low-fat 'butter' spread
- 60ml balsamic vinegar
- 2 tsp brown sugar
- 600-800ml vegetable stock
- 2 tbsp extra virgin olive oil
- 2 tbsp fresh rosemary, chopped
- Salt & pepper for seasoning

Method

ONE
Add all the ingredients, except the olive oil, rosemary and seasoning to your soup maker - making sure not to exceed the maximum fill line.

TWO
Combine all ingredients with a wooden spoon. Once done, place the lid on the soup maker and select the chunky setting.

THREE
Three minutes before the end of the cooking time pause the cycle and add the 'butter'. If your soup maker doesn't have a pause function just add at the end, stir and warm through.

FOUR
When the soup is ready, swirl in the olive oil and sprinkle with fresh rosemary. Season and serve.

CHUNKY KALE SOUP

SERVES 4
chunky

Calories: 125 | **Protein: 4g** | **Fat: 1g** | **Carbs: 26g** | **Fibre: 5g**

Ingredients

- 1 medium onion, chopped
- 1 medium potato, chopped
- 1 medium carrot, chopped
- 50g kale, chopped
- 100g soup pasta
- 1 tsp dried thyme
- 1 tsp dried rosemary
- 2 garlic cloves, sliced
- 600-800ml vegetable stock
- Salt & pepper for seasoning

Method

ONE
Add all the ingredients, except the seasoning to your soup maker - making sure not to exceed the maximum fill line.

TWO
Combine all ingredients with a wooden spoon.

THREE
Secure the lid on the soup maker and select the chunky setting.

FOUR
When the soup is ready, season and serve.

CARROT & APPLE SOUP

Calories: 115 | **Protein: 2g** | **Fat: 1g** | **Carbs: 28g** | **Fibre: 5g**

Ingredients

- 1 medium onion, chopped
- 3 medium carrots, chopped
- 2 green apples, cored & chopped
- 1 tsp ground cinnamon
- ½ tsp ground nutmeg
- 2 garlic cloves, sliced
- 600-800ml vegetable stock
- 1 tbsp honey
- Salt & pepper for seasoning

Method

ONE
Add all the ingredients, except the honey and seasoning, to your soup maker - making sure not to exceed the maximum fill line.

TWO
Combine all ingredients with a wooden spoon.

THREE
Secure the lid on the soup maker and select the smooth setting.

FOUR
When the soup is ready drizzle over the honey, season and serve.

CELERY & BLACK PEPPER SOUP

SERVES 4
⚙ chunky

Calories: 82 | **Protein: 3g** | **Fat: 1g** | **Carbs: 17g** | **Fibre: 3g**

Ingredients

- 4 celery stalks, sliced
- 1 medium onion, chopped
- 1 medium potato, chopped
- 1 tsp ground black pepper
- 2 garlic cloves, sliced
- 500-700ml vegetable stock
- 100ml semi-skimmed milk
- Salt & pepper for seasoning

Method

ONE
Add all the ingredients, except the milk and seasoning to your soup maker - making sure not to exceed the maximum fill line.

TWO
Combine all ingredients with a wooden spoon.

THREE
Secure the lid on the soup maker and select the chunky setting.

FOUR
When the soup is ready stir through the milk, season and serve.

HONEY CABBAGE SOUP

SERVES 4
● chunky

Calories: 91 | **Protein: 2g** | **Fat: 1g** | **Carbs: 20g** | **Fibre: 4g**

Ingredients

- 1 medium onion, chopped
- 1 medium carrot, chopped
- 1 sweetheart/pointed cabbage, chopped
- 1 tsp dried thyme
- 1 tsp dried oregano
- 1 garlic clove, sliced
- 600-800ml vegetable stock
- 2 tbsp honey
- Salt & pepper for seasoning

Method

ONE
Add all the ingredients, except the honey and seasoning to your soup maker - making sure not to exceed the maximum fill line.

TWO
Combine all ingredients with a wooden spoon.

THREE
Secure the lid on the soup maker and select the chunky setting.

FOUR
When the soup is ready, drizzle with honey. Season and serve.

CREAMY TOMATO SOUP

SERVES 4
smooth

| Calories: 96 | Protein: 4g | Fat: 2g | Carbs: 18g | Fibre: 4g |

Ingredients

- 1 medium onion, chopped
- 1 medium carrot, chopped
- 1 tin (400g) chopped tomatoes
- 1 carton (500g) tomato passata
- 2 garlic cloves, sliced
- 1 tsp brown sugar
- 100-200ml semi-skimmed milk
- 4 tbsp fresh basil, chopped
- Salt & pepper for seasoning

Method

ONE
Add all the ingredients, except the milk, basil and seasoning to your soup maker - making sure not to exceed the maximum fill line.

TWO
Combine all ingredients with a wooden spoon.

THREE
Secure the lid on the soup maker and select the smooth setting.

FOUR
When the soup is ready stir through the milk and sprinkle with basil. Season and serve.

BROAD BEAN & MINT SOUP

SERVES 4
⚫ chunky

Calories: 112 | **Protein: 5g** | **Fat: 5g** | **Carbs: 14g** | **Fibre: 6g**

Ingredients

- 1 medium onion, chopped
- 1 medium potato, chopped
- 300g frozen broad beans
- 600-800ml vegetable stock
- 4 tbsp fresh mint, chopped
- 2 tbsp extra virgin olive oil
- Salt & pepper for seasoning

Method

ONE
Add all the ingredients, except the fresh mint, olive oil and seasoning to your soup maker - making sure not to exceed the maximum fill line.

TWO
Combine all ingredients with a wooden spoon. Once done, place the lid on the soup maker and select the chunky setting.

THREE
Three minutes before the end of the cooking time pause the cycle and add the mint. If your soup maker doesn't have a pause function just add at the end, stir and warm through.

FOUR
When the soup is ready, swirl in the olive oil. Season and serve.

LEEK & MUSHROOM SOUP

SERVES 4
● smooth

Calories: 93 | **Protein: 4g** | **Fat: 2g** | **Carbs: 16g** | **Fibre: 3g**

Ingredients

- 2 leeks, sliced
- 1 medium potato, chopped
- 150g mushrooms, sliced
- 2 garlic cloves, sliced
- 600ml-800ml vegetable stock
- 4 tbsp fresh flat leaf parsley, chopped
- Salt & pepper for seasoning

Method

ONE
Add all the ingredients, except the parsley and seasoning, to your soup maker - making sure not to exceed the maximum fill line.

TWO
Combine all ingredients with a wooden spoon.

THREE
Secure the lid on the soup maker and select the smooth setting.

FOUR
When the soup is ready sprinkle with parsley, season and serve.

AVOCADO-TOPPED SPINACH SOUP

SERVES 4
● smooth

Calories: 140 | **Protein: 3g** | **Fat: 11g** | **Carbs: 9g** | **Fibre: 5g**

Ingredients

- 1 medium onion, chopped
- 200g spinach
- 2 garlic cloves, sliced
- ½ tsp ground nutmeg
- 400ml-600ml vegetable stock
- 200ml low-fat coconut milk
- 1 medium ripe avocado, diced
- 1 tsp crushed chilli flakes
- Salt & pepper for seasoning

Method

ONE
Add all the ingredients, except the coconut milk, avocado, chilli flakes and seasoning, to your soup maker - making sure not to exceed the maximum fill line.

TWO
Combine all ingredients with a wooden spoon. Once done, place the lid on the soup maker and select the smooth setting.

THREE
Five minutes before the end of the cooking time pause the cycle and add the coconut milk. If your soup maker doesn't have a pause function just add at the end, stir and warm through.

FOUR
When the soup is ready top with diced avocado, sprinkle with chilli flakes, season and serve.

CARROT & GINGER SOUP

SERVES 4
● smooth

Calories: 108 | **Protein: 2g** | **Fat: 6g** | **Carbs: 13g** | **Fibre: 4g**

Ingredients

- 1 medium onion, chopped
- 4 medium carrots, chopped
- 1 tbsp fresh ginger, grated
- 1 garlic clove, sliced
- 600-800ml vegetable stock
- 2 tbsp extra virgin olive oil
- Salt & pepper for seasoning

Method

ONE
Add all the ingredients, except the olive oil and seasoning, to your soup maker - making sure not to exceed the maximum fill line.

TWO
Combine all ingredients with a wooden spoon.

THREE
Secure the lid on the soup maker and select the smooth setting.

FOUR
When the soup is ready drizzle over the olive oil, season and serve.

CREAMY MUSHROOM SOUP

SERVES 4
● smooth

Calories: 94 | **Protein: 4g** | **Fat: 4g** | **Carbs: 13g** | **Fibre: 3g**

Ingredients

- 1 medium onion, chopped
- 300g mushrooms, sliced
- 1 tsp dried thyme
- 2 garlic cloves, sliced
- 500-700ml vegetable stock
- 100ml low-fat single cream
- Salt & pepper for seasoning

Method

ONE
Add all the ingredients, except the cream and seasoning, to your soup maker - making sure not to exceed the maximum fill line.

TWO
Combine all ingredients with a wooden spoon.

THREE
Secure the lid on the soup maker and select the smooth setting.

FOUR
When the soup is ready stir through the cream, season and serve.

CAULIFLOWER & POTATO SOUP

SERVES 4
● smooth

| Calories: 91 | Protein: 4g | Fat: 1g | Carbs: 20g | Fibre: 4g |

Ingredients

- 1 medium onion, chopped
- ½ cauliflower head, chopped
- 2 medium potatoes
- 1 garlic clove, sliced
- 600-800ml vegetable stock
- 4 tbsp fresh flat leaf parsley, chopped
- Salt & pepper for seasoning

Method

ONE
Add all the ingredients, except the parsley and seasoning, to your soup maker - making sure not to exceed the maximum fill line.

TWO
Combine all ingredients with a wooden spoon.

THREE
Secure the lid on the soup maker and select the smooth setting.

FOUR
When the soup is ready stir through, sprinkle with fresh parsley, season and serve.

ROSEMARY & SWEET POTATO SOUP

SERVES 4
● smooth

Calories: 105 | **Protein: 2g** | **Fat: 0g** | **Carbs: 24g** | **Fibre: 4g**

Ingredients

- 1 medium onion, chopped
- 2 medium sweet potatoes, chopped
- 2 garlic cloves, sliced
- 600-800ml vegetable stock
- 4 tbsp fresh rosemary, chopped
- Salt & pepper for seasoning

Method

ONE
Add all the ingredients, except the rosemary and seasoning, to your soup maker - making sure not to exceed the maximum fill line.

TWO
Combine all ingredients with a wooden spoon.

THREE
Secure the lid on the soup maker and select the smooth setting.

FOUR
When the soup is ready, stir through. Sprinkle with fresh rosemary, season and serve.

BROCCOLI SOUP

SERVES 4
●smooth

| Calories: 66 | Protein: 3g | Fat: 1g | Carbs: 12g | Fibre: 5g |

Ingredients

- 1 medium onion, chopped
- 1 broccoli head, chopped
- 2 garlic cloves, sliced
- 600-800ml vegetable stock
- 1 broccoli stem, very finely chopped
- 2 tbsp poppy seeds
- Salt & pepper for seasoning

Method

ONE
Add all the ingredients, except the chopped broccoli stem, poppy seeds and seasoning, to your soup maker - making sure not to exceed the maximum fill line.

TWO
Combine all ingredients with a wooden spoon.

THREE
Secure the lid on the soup maker and select the smooth setting.

FOUR
When the soup is ready, stir through. Sprinkle soup with the finely chopped broccoli stem and poppy seeds. Season and serve.

CARROT & CAULIFLOWER SOUP

SERVES 4
● smooth

| Calories: 64 | Protein: 3g | Fat: 0g | Carbs: 13g | Fibre: 4g |

Ingredients

- ½ medium onion, chopped
- 2 medium carrots, chopped
- 1 cauliflower head, chopped
- ½ tsp ground cumin
- 1 tsp ground turmeric
- 2 garlic cloves, sliced
- 500-700ml vegetable stock
- Salt & pepper for seasoning

Method

ONE
Add all the ingredients, except the seasoning, to your soup maker - making sure not to exceed the maximum fill line.

TWO
Combine all ingredients with a wooden spoon.

THREE
Secure the lid on the soup maker and select the smooth setting.

FOUR
When the soup is ready, season and serve.

SPICY THREE BEAN SOUP

SERVES 4
😋 chunky

Calories: 149 | **Protein: 6g** | **Fat: 3g** | **Carbs: 26g** | **Fibre: 7g**

Ingredients

- 1 medium onion, chopped
- 1 red pepper, chopped
- 1 tin (390g) three bean salad, rinsed
- 1 tin (400g) chopped tomatoes
- 1 tsp medium chilli powder
- 1 tsp ground cumin
- ½ tsp paprika
- 1 garlic clove, sliced
- 300-500ml vegetable stock
- 50g tortilla chips
- Salt & pepper for seasoning

Method

ONE
Add all the ingredients, except the tortilla chips and seasoning to your soup maker - making sure not to exceed the maximum fill line.

TWO
Combine all ingredients with a wooden spoon.

THREE
Secure the lid on the soup maker and select the chunky setting.

FOUR
When the soup is ready smash the tortilla chips and sprinkle over the top of each soup bowl. Season and serve.

CHUNKY VEGETABLE SOUP

Calories: 96 | **Protein: 3g** | **Fat: 1g** | **Carbs: 20g** | **Fibre: 5g**

Ingredients

- 1 medium onion, chopped
- 1 medium carrot, chopped
- 1 medium potato, chopped
- 1 celery stalk, sliced
- 50g green beans, chopped
- 1 tin (400g) chopped tomatoes
- 1 tsp dried thyme
- 1 tsp dried oregano
- 2 garlic cloves, sliced
- 400-600ml vegetable stock
- Salt & pepper for seasoning

Method

ONE
Add all the ingredients, except the seasoning to your soup maker - making sure not to exceed the maximum fill line.

TWO
Combine all ingredients with a wooden spoon.

THREE
Secure the lid on the soup maker and select the chunky setting.

FOUR
When the soup is ready, season and serve.

GINGER & PARSNIP SOUP

SERVES 4
●smooth

Calories: 131 | **Protein: 2g** | **Fat: 4g** | **Carbs: 24g** | **Fibre: 6g**

Ingredients

- 1 medium onion, chopped
- 1 medium carrot, chopped
- 2 medium parsnips, finely chopped
- 1 tbsp fresh ginger, grated
- 1 tbsp ground turmeric
- ½ tsp ground nutmeg
- 1 garlic clove, sliced
- 500-700ml vegetable stock
- 100ml low-fat coconut milk
- 4 tbsp fresh coriander, chopped
- Salt & pepper for seasoning

Method

ONE
Add all the ingredients, except the coconut milk, coriander and seasoning to your soup maker - making sure not to exceed the maximum fill line.

TWO
Combine all ingredients with a wooden spoon.

THREE
Secure the lid on the soup maker and select the smooth setting.

FOUR
When the soup is ready stir through the coconut milk and sprinkle with fresh coriander. Season and serve.

FRESH HERB POTATO SOUP

SERVES 4
●smooth

Calories: 104 | **Protein: 3g** | **Fat: 2g** | **Carbs: 19g** | **Fibre: 4g**

Ingredients

- 1 medium onion, chopped
- 3 medium potatoes, chopped
- 2 garlic cloves, sliced
- 500-700ml vegetable stock
- 100ml low-fat single cream
- Large bunch of mixed fresh herbs (chives, parsley & dill), chopped
- Salt & pepper for seasoning

Method

ONE
Add all the ingredients, except the cream, fresh herbs and seasoning, to your soup maker - making sure not to exceed the maximum fill line.

TWO
Combine all ingredients with a wooden spoon.

THREE
Secure the lid on the soup maker and select the smooth setting.

FOUR
When the soup is ready swirl in the single cream and pile the chopped fresh herbs on top. Season and serve.

CHIPOTLE SQUASH SOUP

SERVES 4
● smooth

Calories: 106 | **Protein: 3g** | **Fat: 3g** | **Carbs: 19g** | **Fibre: 4g**

Ingredients

- 1 medium onion, chopped
- 1 medium butternut squash, peeled & chopped
- 1 garlic clove, sliced
- 1 tbsp chipotle paste
- 500-700ml vegetable stock
- 100ml low-fat single cream
- 4 tbsp fresh coriander, chopped
- 1 lime, quartered
- Salt & pepper for seasoning

Method

ONE
Add all the ingredients, except the cream, coriander, lime and seasoning, to your soup maker - making sure not to exceed the maximum fill line.

TWO
Combine all ingredients with a wooden spoon.

THREE
Secure the lid on the soup maker and select the smooth setting.

FOUR
When the soup is ready, stir in the single cream. Season and serve with a lime wedge on the side.

BROCCOLI & COCONUT SOUP

SERVES 4
● smooth

Calories: 136 | **Protein: 4g** | **Fat: 7g** | **Carbs: 17g** | **Fibre: 5g**

Ingredients

- 1 medium leek, sliced
- 1 medium carrot, chopped
- 1 broccoli head, chopped
- 1 tbsp medium curry powder
- ½ tsp ground cumin
- 1 garlic clove, sliced
- 500-700ml vegetable stock
- 100ml low-fat coconut milk
- 4 tbsp peanuts, chopped (optional)
- Salt & pepper for seasoning

Method

ONE
Add all the ingredients, except the coconut milk, peanuts and seasoning, to your soup maker - making sure not to exceed the maximum fill line.

TWO
Combine all ingredients with a wooden spoon. Once done, place the lid on the soup maker and select the smooth setting.

THREE
Three minutes before the end of the cooking time pause the cycle and add the coconut milk. If your soup maker doesn't have a pause function just add at the end, stir and warm through.

FOUR
When the soup is ready, top with chopped peanuts. Season and serve.

VEGETABLE MINESTRONE SOUP

SERVES 4
⚙ chunky

Calories: 124 | **Protein: 4g** | **Fat: 1g** | **Carbs: 25g** | **Fibre: 5g**

Ingredients

- 1 medium onion, chopped
- 1 medium carrot, chopped
- 1 medium courgette, chopped
- 1 celery stalk, sliced
- ½ tin (200g) cannellini beans, rinsed
- 50g soup pasta
- 1 tsp dried basil
- 1 tsp dried oregano
- 2 garlic cloves, sliced
- 500-700ml vegetable stock
- Salt & pepper for seasoning

Method

ONE
Add all the ingredients, except the seasoning to your soup maker - making sure not to exceed the maximum fill line.

TWO
Combine all ingredients with a wooden spoon.

THREE
Secure the lid on the soup maker and select the chunky setting.

FOUR
When the soup is ready, season and serve.

CURRIED CARROT SOUP

SERVES 4
● smooth

Calories: 134 | **Protein: 3g** | **Fat: 7g** | **Carbs: 16g** | **Fibre: 4g**

Ingredients

- 1 medium onion, chopped
- 4 medium carrots, chopped
- 1 tbsp medium curry powder
- 2 garlic cloves, sliced
- 400-600ml vegetable stock
- 200ml low-fat coconut milk
- 2 tbsp coconut flakes
- Salt & pepper for seasoning

Method

ONE
Add all the ingredients, except the coconut milk, flakes and seasoning, to your soup maker - making sure not to exceed the maximum fill line.

TWO
Combine all ingredients with a wooden spoon. Once done, place the lid on the soup maker and select the smooth setting.

THREE
Three minutes before the end of the cooking time pause the cycle and add the coconut milk. If your soup maker doesn't have a pause function just add at the end, stir and warm through.

FOUR
When the soup is ready sprinkle with coconut flakes, season and serve.

RICE & VEGETABLE SOUP

SERVES 4
● chunky

Calories: 118 | Protein: 3g | Fat: 1g | Carbs: 25g | Fibre: 4g

Ingredients

- 1 medium onion, chopped
- 2 medium carrots, chopped
- 1 medium courgette, chopped
- 1 celery stalk, sliced
- ½ pack (125g) pre-cooked white rice
- 1 tin (400g) chopped tomatoes
- 1 tsp dried rosemary
- 1 tsp dried thyme
- 2 garlic cloves, sliced
- 300-500ml vegetable stock
- 4 tbsp fresh parsley, chopped
- Salt & pepper for seasoning

Method

ONE
Add all the ingredients, except the parsley and seasoning to your soup maker - making sure not to exceed the maximum fill line.

TWO
Combine all ingredients with a wooden spoon.

THREE
Secure the lid on the soup maker and select the chunky setting.

FOUR
When the soup is ready sprinkle with parsley, season and serve.

PARSNIP & BLUE CHEESE SOUP

SERVES 4
● smooth

Calories: 168 | **Protein: 5g** | **Fat: 10g** | **Carbs: 17g** | **Fibre: 4g**

Ingredients

- 1 medium onion, chopped
- 1 medium parsnip, finely chopped
- 2 ripe pears, cored and chopped
- ½ tsp ground nutmeg
- 1 garlic clove, sliced
- 600-800ml vegetable stock
- 75g blue cheese, crumbled
- 4 tbsp raw walnuts, chopped (optional)
- Salt & pepper for seasoning

Method

ONE
Add all the ingredients, except the blue cheese, walnuts and seasoning to your soup maker - making sure not to exceed the maximum fill line.

TWO
Combine all ingredients with a wooden spoon.

THREE
Secure the lid on the soup maker and select the smooth setting.

FOUR
When the soup is ready stir through the cheese until melted. Sprinkle with walnuts, season and serve.

CREAMY SPINACH SOUP

SERVES 4
smooth

Calories: 98 | **Protein: 4g** | **Fat: 2g** | **Carbs: 17g** | **Fibre: 4g**

Ingredients

- 1 medium onion, chopped
- 1 medium potato, chopped
- 100g frozen peas
- 75g spinach
- 2 tsp medium curry powder
- ½ tsp ground nutmeg
- 1 garlic clove, sliced
- 500-700ml vegetable stock
- 100ml low-fat single cream
- Salt & pepper for seasoning

Method

ONE
Add all the ingredients, except the cream and seasoning, to your soup maker - making sure not to exceed the maximum fill line.

TWO
Combine all ingredients with a wooden spoon.

THREE
Secure the lid on the soup maker and select the smooth setting.

FOUR
When the soup is ready stir through the cream, season and serve.

PEA SOUP

SERVES 4
● smooth

Calories: 134	Protein: 4g	Fat: 4g	Carbs: 21g	Fibre: 5g

Ingredients

- 1 medium onion, chopped
- 1 medium potato, chopped
- 300g frozen peas
- 1 garlic clove, sliced
- 600-800ml vegetable stock
- 2 tbsp extra virgin olive oil
- Salt & pepper for seasoning

Method

ONE
Add all the ingredients, except the oil and seasoning, to your soup maker - making sure not to exceed the maximum fill line.

TWO
Combine all ingredients with a wooden spoon.

THREE
Secure the lid on the soup maker and select the smooth setting.

FOUR
When the soup is ready stir through the olive oil, season and serve.

CURRIED CAULIFLOWER SOUP

SERVES 4
⬤ smooth

Calories: 89 | **Protein: 4g** | **Fat: 3g** | **Carbs: 13g** | **Fibre: 4g**

Ingredients

- 1 medium onion, chopped
- 1 cauliflower head, chopped
- 2 garlic cloves, sliced
- 1 tbsp medium curry powder
- 1 tsp ground cumin
- 600-800ml vegetable stock
- 3 tbsp toasted pecan nuts, chopped (optional)
- 4 tbsp fresh coriander, chopped
- Salt & pepper for seasoning

Method

ONE
Add all the ingredients, except the pecans, coriander and seasoning, to your soup maker - making sure not to exceed the maximum fill line.

TWO
Combine all ingredients with a wooden spoon.

THREE
Secure the lid on the soup maker and select the smooth setting.

FOUR
When the soup is ready sprinkle with pecans and fresh coriander. Season and serve.

MAPLE SWEET POTATO SOUP

SERVES 4
● smooth

Calories: 113 | **Protein: 2g** | **Fat: 1g** | **Carbs: 27g** | **Fibre: 4g**

Ingredients

- 1 medium onion, chopped
- 2 medium sweet potatoes, chopped
- 1 tsp ground cinnamon
- ½ tsp ground nutmeg
- 1 garlic clove, sliced
- 600-800ml vegetable stock
- 2 tbsp maple syrup
- Salt & pepper for seasoning

Method

ONE
Add all the ingredients, except the maple syrup and seasoning, to your soup maker - making sure not to exceed the maximum fill line.

TWO
Combine all ingredients with a wooden spoon.

THREE
Secure the lid on the soup maker and select the smooth setting.

FOUR
When the soup is ready drizzle each bowl with maple syrup, season and serve.

ITALIAN LENTIL SOUP

SERVES 4
● smooth

Calories: 103 | Protein: 6g | Fat: 1g | Carbs: 18g | Fibre: 6g

Ingredients

- 1 medium onion, chopped
- 1 medium carrot, chopped
- 1 tin (390g) cooked lentils, rinsed
- ½ tln (200g) chopped tomatoes
- 1 tsp dried oregano
- 1 tsp dried thyme
- 2 garlic cloves, sliced
- 400-600ml vegetable stock
- 2 tbsp Parmesan cheese, grated
- Salt & pepper for seasoning

Method

ONE
Add all the ingredients, except the Parmesan cheese and seasoning, to your soup maker - making sure not to exceed the maximum fill line.

TWO
Combine all ingredients with a wooden spoon.

THREE
Secure the lid on the soup maker and select the smooth setting.

FOUR
When the soup is ready sprinkle with Parmesan, season and serve.

MUSHROOM MISO SOUP

SERVES 4
chunky

Calories: 68 | **Protein: 4g** | **Fat: 3g** | **Carbs: 8g** | **Fibre: 2g**

Ingredients

- 1 medium onion, chopped
- 200g mushrooms, sliced
- 100g tofu
- 2 garlic cloves, sliced
- 1 tbsp fresh ginger, grated
- 1 tbsp soy sauce
- 1 tbsp miso paste
- 600-800ml water
- 4 spring onions, finely sliced
- Salt & pepper for seasoning

Method

ONE
Add all the ingredients, except the spring onions and seasoning, to your soup maker - making sure not to exceed the maximum fill line.

TWO
Combine all ingredients with a wooden spoon.

THREE
Secure the lid on the soup maker and select the chunky setting.

FOUR
When the soup is ready top with spring onions, season and serve.

CARROT & CASHEW SOUP

SERVES 4
● smooth

Calories: 147 | **Protein: 4g** | **Fat: 9g** | **Carbs: 14g** | **Fibre: 3g**

Ingredients

- 1 medium onion, chopped
- 4 medium carrots, chopped
- 100g raw cashew nuts
- 1 tsp ground cumin
- 1 garllc clove, sllced
- 600-800ml vegetable stock
- 2 tbsp toasted cashew nuts, chopped
- Salt & pepper for seasoning

Method

ONE
Add all the ingredients, except the toasted cashew nuts and seasoning, to your soup maker - making sure not to exceed the maximum fill line.

TWO
Combine all ingredients with a wooden spoon.

THREE
Secure the lid on the soup maker and select the smooth setting.

FOUR
When the soup is ready sprinkle with the toasted cashews, season and serve.

CHICKPEA SOUP

SERVES 4
 smooth

| Calories: 124 | Protein: 6g | Fat: 2g | Carbs: 22g | Fibre: 5g |

Ingredients

- 1 medium onion, chopped
- 1 medium carrot, chopped
- 1 tin (390g) chickpeas, rinsed
- 1 garlic clove, sliced
- 1 tsp ground cumin
- ½ tsp ground coriander
- ½ tsp crushed chilli flakes
- 1 garlic clove, sliced
- 500-700ml vegetable stock
- 2 tbsp lemon juice
- Salt & pepper for seasoning

Method

ONE
Add all the ingredients, except the lemon juice seasoning to your soup maker - making sure not to exceed the maximum fill line.

TWO
Combine all ingredients with a wooden spoon.

THREE
Secure the lid on the soup maker and select the smooth setting.

FOUR
When the soup is ready, stir through the lemon juice, season and serve.

LEEK & LENTIL SOUP

SERVES 4
●smooth

| Calories: 104 | Protein: 6g | Fat: 1g | Carbs: 19g | Fibre: 6g |

Ingredients

- 2 leeks, sliced
- 1 tin (390g) cooked lentils, rinsed
- 1 medium carrot, chopped
- 1 tsp dried thyme
- 500ml-700ml vegetable stock
- Salt & pepper for seasoning

Method

ONE
Add all the ingredients, except the seasoning to your soup maker - making sure not to exceed the maximum fill line.

TWO
Combine all ingredients with a wooden spoon.

THREE
Secure the lid on the soup maker and select the smooth setting.

FOUR
When the soup is ready season and serve.

CREAMY LEEK & CHICKPEA SOUP

SERVES 4
● smooth

Calories: 136 | Protein: 6g | Fat: 6g | Carbs: 16g | Fibre: 5g

Ingredients

- 2 leeks, sliced
- 1 tin (390g) chickpeas, rinsed
- 2 garlic cloves, sliced
- 1 tsp dried basil
- 600ml-800ml vegetable stock
- 2 tbsp olive oil
- Salt & pepper for seasoning

Method

ONE
Add all the ingredients, except the olive oil and seasoning, to your soup maker - making sure not to exceed the maximum fill line.

TWO
Combine all ingredients with a wooden spoon.

THREE
Secure the lid on the soup maker and select the smooth setting.

FOUR
When the soup is ready drizzle with olive oil, season and serve.

AVOCADO-TOPPED CARROT SOUP

SERVES 4
● smooth

Calories: 117 | **Protein: 2g** | **Fat: 8g** | **Carbs: 12g** | **Fibre: 5g**

Ingredients

- 1 medium onion, chopped
- 4 medium carrots, chopped
- 2 garlic cloves, sliced
- 600ml-800ml vegetable stock
- 1 medium ripe avocado, diced
- Salt & pepper for seasoning

Method

ONE
Add all the ingredients, except the avocado and seasoning, to your soup maker - making sure not to exceed the maximum fill line.

TWO
Combine all ingredients with a wooden spoon.

THREE
Secure the lid on the soup maker and select the smooth setting.

FOUR
When the soup is ready top with diced avocado, season and serve.

SIMPLE LENTIL SOUP

Calories: 113 | **Protein: 6g** | **Fat: 1g** | **Carbs: 21g** | **Fibre: 6g**

Ingredients

- 1 medium onion, chopped
- 2 medium carrots, chopped
- 1 tin (390g) cooked lentils, rinsed
- 1 tsp ground cumin
- 1 garlic clove, sliced
- 500-700ml vegetable stock
- Salt & pepper for seasoning

Method

ONE
Add all the ingredients, except the seasoning to your soup maker - making sure not to exceed the maximum fill line.

TWO
Combine all ingredients with a wooden spoon.

THREE
Secure the lid on the soup maker and select the smooth setting.

FOUR
When the soup is ready, season and serve.

SPINACH & PARMESAN SOUP

SERVES 4
● smooth

Calories: 116 | **Protein: 5g** | **Fat: 4g** | **Carbs: 16g** | **Fibre: 4g**

Ingredients

- 1 leek, sliced
- 2 medium potatoes, chopped
- 2 garlic cloves, sliced
- 100g spinach
- 600ml-800ml vegetable stock
- 4 tbsp Parmesan cheese, grated
- Salt & pepper for seasoning

Method

ONE
Add all the ingredients, except the Parmesan cheese and seasoning, to your soup maker - making sure not to exceed the maximum fill line.

TWO
Combine all ingredients with a wooden spoon.

THREE
Secure the lid on the soup maker and select the smooth setting.

FOUR
When the soup is ready sprinkle over the Parmesan cheese, season and serve.

ZESTY CORIANDER SOUP

SERVES 4
● smooth

Calories: 103 | Protein: 3g | Fat: 1g | Carbs: 21g | Fibre: 4g

Ingredients

- 2 leeks, sliced
- 2 medium potatoes, chopped
- 2 garlic cloves, sliced
- 1 bunch fresh coriander, chopped
- 600ml-800ml vegetable stock
- 4 tbsp low-fat Greek yoghurt
- Zest of 1 lime
- Salt & pepper for seasoning

Method

ONE
Add all the ingredients, except the yoghurt, lime zest and seasoning, to your soup maker - making sure not to exceed the maximum fill line.

TWO
Combine all ingredients with a wooden spoon.

THREE
Secure the lid on the soup maker and select the smooth setting.

FOUR
When the soup is ready dollop the yoghurt into the centre of each bowl and sprinkle the zest on top. Season and serve.

CREAM OF CHICKEN SOUP

SERVES 4
smooth

Calories: 275 | **Protein: 23g** | **Fat: 6g** | **Carbs: 28g** | **Fibre: 3g**

Ingredients

- 1 medium onion, chopped
- 1 medium carrot, chopped
- 1 medium potato, chopped
- 300g cooked chicken, shredded
- 1 garlic clove, sliced
- 500-600ml chicken stock
- 200ml semi-skimmed milk
- 4 tbsp fresh flat leaf parsley, chopped
- Salt & pepper for seasoning

Method

ONE
Add all the ingredients, except the milk, parsley and seasoning, to your soup maker - making sure not to exceed the maximum fill line.

TWO
Combine all ingredients with a wooden spoon. Once done, place the lid on the soup maker and select the smooth setting.

THREE
Three minutes before the end of the cooking time pause the cycle and add the milk. If your soup maker doesn't have a pause function just add at the end, stir and warm through.

FOUR
When the soup is ready, season and serve with chopped parsley sprinkled over the top of each bowl.

BEEF & RED ONION SOUP

SERVES 4
chunky

Calories: 320 | **Protein: 25g** | **Fat: 12g** | **Carbs: 25g** | **Fibre: 4g**

Ingredients

- 1 medium red onion, chopped
- 1 medium carrot, chopped
- 1 medium potato, chopped
- 1 tin (400g) chopped tomatoes
- 1 garlic clove, sliced
- 600ml-800ml beef stock
- 200g cooked beef, chopped
- 4 tbsp fresh basil, chopped
- Salt & pepper for seasoning

Method

ONE
Add all the ingredients, except the beef, basil and seasoning, to your soup maker - making sure not to exceed the maximum fill line.

TWO
Combine all ingredients with a wooden spoon. Once done, place the lid on the soup maker and select the chunky setting.

THREE
Five minutes before the end of the cooking time pause the cycle and add the beef and basil. If your soup maker doesn't have a pause function just add at the end, stir and warm through.

FOUR
When the soup is ready, season and serve.

LAMB & PUMPKIN SOUP

SERVES 4
chunky

Calories: 330 | Protein: 24g | Fat: 13g | Carbs: 25g | Fibre: 4g

Ingredients

- 1 medium onion, chopped
- 1 celery stalk, sliced
- 200g pumpkin flesh, diced
- 1 garlic clove, sliced
- 1 tsp dried rosemary
- 600ml-800ml chicken or lamb stock
- 200g cooked roast lamb, chopped
- 1 tbsp pumpkin seeds, chopped
- Salt & pepper for seasoning

Method

ONE
Add all the ingredients, except the lamb, pumpkin seeds and seasoning, to your soup maker - making sure not to exceed the maximum fill line.

TWO
Combine all ingredients with a wooden spoon. Once done, place the lid on the soup maker and select the chunky setting.

THREE
Five minutes before the end of the cooking time pause the cycle and add the lamb. If your soup maker doesn't have a pause function just add at the end, stir and warm through.

FOUR
When the soup is ready sprinkle over the pumpkin seeds, season and serve.

CHICKEN & SPRING ONION SOUP

SERVES 4
🍪 chunky

Calories: 365 | Protein: 25g | Fat: 18g | Carbs: 25g | Fibre: 4g

Ingredients

- 1 medium onion, chopped
- 1 medium sweet potato, chopped
- 1 medium carrot, chopped
- 2 garlic cloves, sliced
- 500-700ml chicken stock
- 200g cooked chicken, shredded
- 100ml coconut milk
- 4 spring onions, finely sliced
- Salt & pepper for seasoning

Method

ONE
Add all the ingredients, except the chicken, coconut milk, spring onions and seasoning, to your soup maker - making sure not to exceed the maximum fill line.

TWO
Combine all ingredients with a wooden spoon. Once done, place the lid on the soup maker and select the chunky setting.

THREE
Five minutes before the end of the cooking time pause the cycle to add the chicken and coconut milk. If your soup maker doesn't have a pause function just add at the end, stir and warm through.

FOUR
When the soup is ready, season and serve with finely sliced spring onions sprinkled over the top of each bowl.

SCOTCH BARLEY BROTH

SERVES 4
chunky

Calories: 380 | **Protein: 27g** | **Fat: 11g** | **Carbs: 43g** | **Fibre: 6g**

Ingredients

- 1 medium onion, chopped
- 1 medium carrot, chopped
- 1 medium potato, chopped
- 150g pre-cooked pearl barley
- 4 tbsp fresh flat leaf parsley, chopped
- 600-800ml beef stock
- 300g cooked lamb, chopped
- Salt & pepper for seasoning

Method

ONE
Add all the ingredients, except the lamb and seasoning, to your soup maker - making sure not to exceed the maximum fill line.

TWO
Combine all ingredients with a wooden spoon. Once done, place the lid on the soup maker and select the chunky setting.

THREE
Five minutes before the end of the cooking time pause the cycle and add the lamb. If your soup maker doesn't have a pause function just add at the end, stir and warm through.

FOUR
When the soup is ready, season and serve.

CHICKEN & MUSHROOM SOUP

SERVES 4
😋 chunky

Calories: 220 | Protein: 22g | Fat: 4g | Carbs: 22g | Fibre: 3g

Ingredients

- 1 medium onion, chopped
- 1 medium potato, chopped
- 200g shitake mushrooms, sliced
- 1 garlic clove, sliced
- 600-800ml chicken stock
- 200g cooked chicken, shredded
- 2 tbsp fresh thyme, chopped
- Zest from 1 lemon
- Salt & pepper for seasoning

Method

ONE
Add all the ingredients, except the chicken, fresh thyme, lemon zest and seasoning, to your soup maker - making sure not to exceed the maximum fill line.

TWO
Combine all ingredients with a wooden spoon. Once done, place the lid on the soup maker and select the chunky setting.

THREE
Five minutes before the end of the cooking time pause the cycle and add the chicken. If your soup maker doesn't have a pause function just add at the end, stir and warm through.

FOUR
When the soup is ready, season and serve with fresh thyme and lemon zest sprinkled over the top of each bowl.

WHITE BEAN & BACON SOUP

SERVES 4
chunky

Calories: 345 | **Protein: 23g** | **Fat: 11g** | **Carbs: 37g** | **Fibre: 9g**

Ingredients

- 1 medium onion, chopped
- 1 medium carrot, chopped
- 1 tin (390g) cannellini beans, rinsed
- 1 tsp paprika
- 600-800ml beef stock
- 4 rashers cooked bacon, chopped
- 4 tbsp fresh flat leaf parsley, chopped
- Salt & pepper for seasoning

Method

ONE
Add all the ingredients, except the bacon, fresh parsley and seasoning, to your soup maker - making sure not to exceed the maximum fill line.

TWO
Combine all ingredients with a wooden spoon. Once done, place the lid on the soup maker and select the chunky setting.

THREE
Five minutes before the end of the cooking time pause the cycle and add the bacon. If your soup maker doesn't have a pause function just add at the end, stir and warm through.

FOUR
When the soup is ready, season and serve with parsley sprinkled over the top of each bowl.

SMOKY HAM & CELERY SOUP

SERVES 4
chunky

Calories: 290 | **Protein: 24g** | **Fat: 8g** | **Carbs: 31g** | **Fibre: 5g**

Ingredients

- 1 medium onion, chopped
- 1 medium carrot, chopped
- 1 medium sweet potato, chopped
- 100g frozen peas
- 2 garlic cloves, sliced
- 1 tsp smoked paprika
- 600-800ml chicken stock
- 200g thick, chunky cooked ham, chopped
- 2 celery stalks, very finely chopped
- Salt & pepper for seasoning

Method

ONE
Add all the ingredients, except the ham, celery and seasoning, to your soup maker - making sure not to exceed the maximum fill line.

TWO
Combine all ingredients with a wooden spoon. Once done, place the lid on the soup maker and select the chunky setting.

THREE
When the soup is ready add the ham and warm through.

FOUR
Season and serve with the chopped celery sprinkled over the top of each bowl.

BEEF & CHICKPEA SOUP

SERVES 4
chunky

Calories: 345 | **Protein: 30g** | **Fat: 9g** | **Carbs: 34g** | **Fibre: 9g**

Ingredients

- 1 medium onion, chopped
- 2 medium carrots, chopped
- 1 tin (390g) chickpeas, rinsed
- 1 garlic clove, sliced
- 600ml-800ml beef stock
- 200g cooked roast beef, chopped
- Salt & pepper for seasoning

Method

ONE
Add all the ingredients, except the beef and seasoning, to your soup maker - making sure not to exceed the maximum fill line.

TWO
Combine all ingredients with a wooden spoon. Once done, place the lid on the soup maker and select the chunky setting.

THREE
Five minutes before the end of the cooking time pause the cycle and add the beef. If your soup maker doesn't have a pause function just add at the end, stir and warm through.

FOUR
When the soup is ready, season and serve.

MINTED LAMB SOUP

SERVES 4
🍲 chunky

Calories: 330 | **Protein: 28g** | **Fat: 12g** | **Carbs: 28g** | **Fibre: 5g**

Ingredients

- 1 medium carrot, chopped
- 1 medium onion, chopped
- 1 medium potato, chopped
- 1 medium leek, sliced
- 150g frozen peas
- 2 tbsp fresh mint, chopped
- 600-800ml chicken or lamb stock
- 200g cooked lamb, chopped
- 2 garlic cloves, finely chopped
- Zest from 1 lemon
- Salt & pepper for seasoning

Method

ONE
Add all the ingredients, except the lamb, garlic, lemon zest and seasoning, to your soup maker - making sure not to exceed the maximum fill line.

TWO
Combine all ingredients with a wooden spoon. Once done, place the lid on the soup maker and select the chunky setting.

THREE
Five minutes before the end of the cooking time pause the cycle and add the lamb. If your soup maker doesn't have a pause function just add at the end, stir and warm through.

FOUR
When the soup is ready, season and serve with the garlic and lemon zest sprinkled over the top of each bowl.

CHICKEN & CORIANDER SOUP

SERVES 4
● smooth

Calories: 330 | **Protein: 32g** | **Fat: 10g** | **Carbs: 29g** | **Fibre: 4g**

Ingredients

- 1 medium onion, chopped
- 1 medium potato, chopped
- 1 medium carrot, chopped
- 1 garlic clove, sliced
- 1 tbsp medium curry powder
- 600-800ml chicken stock
- 300g cooked chicken, shredded
- 4 tbsp fresh coriander, chopped
- 2 tbsp peanuts, chopped (optional)
- Salt & pepper for seasoning

Method

ONE
Add all the ingredients, except the chicken, fresh coriander, peanuts and seasoning, to your soup maker - making sure not to exceed the maximum fill line.

TWO
Combine all ingredients with a wooden spoon. Once done, place the lid on the soup maker and select the smooth setting.

THREE
Five minutes before the end of the cooking time pause the cycle and add the chicken. If your soup maker doesn't have a pause function just add at the end, stir and warm through.

FOUR
When the soup is ready, season and serve with fresh coriander and chopped peanuts sprinkled over the top of each bowl.

TURKEY & FRESH PEPPER SOUP

SERVES 4
chunky

Calories: 250 | **Protein: 24g** | **Fat: 3g** | **Carbs: 35g** | **Fibre: 6g**

Ingredients

- 1 medium parsnip, finely chopped
- 1 medium carrot, chopped
- 1 medium onion, chopped
- 1 tin (400g) chopped tomatoes
- 1 garlic clove, sliced
- 400-600ml chicken stock
- 1 tbsp honey
- 200g cooked turkey, shredded
- 4 tbsp pomegranate seeds
- 1 red pepper, very finely chopped
- Salt & pepper for seasoning

Method

ONE
Add all the ingredients, except the turkey, pomegranate seeds, red pepper and seasoning, to your soup maker - making sure not to exceed the maximum fill line.

TWO
Combine all ingredients with a wooden spoon. Once done, place the lid on the soup maker and select the chunky setting.

THREE
Five minutes before the end of the cooking time pause the cycle and add the turkey. If your soup maker doesn't have a pause function just add at the end, stir and warm through.

FOUR
When the soup is ready, season and serve with pomegranate seeds and chopped red pepper sprinkled over the top of each bowl.

BEEF & QUINOA SOUP

SERVES 4
⚙ chunky

Calories: 370 | **Protein: 28g** | **Fat: 10g** | **Carbs: 40g** | **Fibre: 6g**

Ingredients

- 1 medium onion, chopped
- 1 medium carrot, chopped
- ½ pack (125g) pre-cooked quinoa
- 2 tbsp soy sauce
- 1 tbsp tomato puree
- 1 garlic clove, sliced
- 1 tsp dried rosemary
- 600-800ml beef stock
- 200g cooked beef, chopped
- Salt & pepper for seasoning

Method

ONE
Add all the ingredients, except the beef and seasoning, to your soup maker - making sure not to exceed the maximum fill line.

TWO
Combine all ingredients with a wooden spoon. Once done, place the lid on the soup maker and select the chunky setting.

THREE
Five minutes before the end of the cooking time pause the cycle and add the beef. If your soup maker doesn't have a pause function just add at the end, stir and warm through.

FOUR
When the soup is ready, season and serve.

CHICKEN & CARROT SOUP

SERVES 4
chunky

Calories: 280 | **Protein: 28g** | **Fat: 5g** | **Carbs: 30g** | **Fibre: 6g**

Ingredients

- 1 medium carrot, chopped
- 1 medium onion, chopped
- 1 medium potato, chopped
- 100g frozen peas
- ½ tsp ground ginger
- 1 tsp paprika
- 600-800ml chicken stock
- 300g cooked chicken, shredded
- 1 medium carrot, grated
- Salt & pepper for seasoning

Method

ONE
Add all the ingredients, except the chicken, grated carrot and seasoning, to your soup maker - making sure not to exceed the maximum fill line.

TWO
Combine all ingredients with a wooden spoon. Once done, place the lid on the soup maker and select the chunky setting.

THREE
Five minutes before the end of the cooking time pause the cycle and add the chicken. If your soup maker doesn't have a pause function just add at the end, stir and warm through.

FOUR
When the soup is ready, season and serve with grated carrot sprinkled over the top of each bowl.

BEEF & ROASTED PEPPER SOUP

SERVES 4
⊕ chunky

Calories: 320 | **Protein: 27g** | **Fat: 10g** | **Carbs: 25g** | **Fibre: 5g**

Ingredients

- 1 medium onion, chopped
- 2 medium carrots, chopped
- 1 celery stalk, sliced
- ¼ jar (100g) roasted red peppers
- 1 tbsp balsamic vinegar
- 600-800ml beef stock
- 200g cooked roast beef, chopped
- Salt & pepper for seasoning

Method

ONE
Add all the ingredients, except the beef and seasoning, to your soup maker - making sure not to exceed the maximum fill line.

TWO
Combine all ingredients with a wooden spoon. Once done, place the lid on the soup maker and select the chunky setting.

THREE
Five minutes before the end of the cooking time pause the cycle and add the beef. If your soup maker doesn't have a pause function just add at the end, stir and warm through.

FOUR
When the soup is ready, season and serve.

PEA & HAM SOUP

SERVES 4
chunky

Calories: 345 | **Protein: 26g** | **Fat: 6g** | **Carbs: 42g** | **Fibre: 10g**

Ingredients

- 1 medium onion, chopped
- 1 medium carrot, chopped
- 1 medium potato, chopped
- 400g frozen peas
- 1 tsp dried oregano
- 600-800ml chicken stock
- 50g spinach, chopped
- 200g thick, chunky cooked ham, chopped
- Zest from 1 lemon
- Salt & pepper for seasoning

Method

ONE
Add all the ingredients, except the spinach, ham, lemon zest and seasoning, to your soup maker - making sure not to exceed the maximum fill line.

TWO
Combine all ingredients with a wooden spoon. Once done, place the lid on the soup maker and select the chunky setting.

THREE
Three minutes before the end of the cooking time pause the cycle and add the spinach. If your soup maker doesn't have a pause function just add at the end, stir and warm through.

FOUR
When the soup is ready add the ham and warm through. Season and serve with lemon zest sprinkled over the top of each bowl.

CHICKEN & SQUASH SOUP

SERVES 4
⚙ chunky

Calories: 260 | **Protein: 23g** | **Fat: 6g** | **Carbs: 28g** | **Fibre: 6g**

Ingredients

- 1 medium onion, chopped
- 1 butternut squash, peeled & chopped
- 1 garlic clove, sliced
- 1 tsp dried thyme
- 600-800ml chicken stock
- 200g cooked chicken, shredded
- 2 tbsp pumpkin seeds, chopped
- Salt & pepper for seasoning

Method

ONE
Add all the ingredients, except the chicken, pumpkin seeds and seasoning, to your soup maker - making sure not to exceed the maximum fill line.

TWO
Combine all ingredients with a wooden spoon, Once done, place the lid on the soup maker and select the chunky setting.

THREE
Five minutes before the end of the cooking time pause the cycle and add the chicken. If your soup maker doesn't have a pause function just add at the end, stir and warm through.

FOUR
When the soup is ready, season and serve with chopped pumpkin seeds sprinkled over the top of each bowl.

BEEF & MUSHROOM SOUP

Calories: 330 | **Protein: 28g** | **Fat: 11g** | **Carbs: 25g** | **Fibre: 5g**

Ingredients

- 1 medium onion, chopped
- 2 medium carrots, chopped
- 200g mushrooms, sliced
- 2 tbsp tomato puree
- 1 garlic clove, sliced
- 1 tsp dried rosemary
- 600-800ml beef stock
- 200g cooked roast beef, chopped
- Salt & pepper for seasoning

Method

ONE
Add all the ingredients, except the beef and seasoning, to your soup maker - making sure not to exceed the maximum fill line.

TWO
Combine all ingredients with a wooden spoon. Once done, place the lid on the soup maker and select the chunky setting.

THREE
Five minutes before the end of the cooking time pause the cycle and add the beef. If your soup maker doesn't have a pause function just add at the end, stir and warm through.

FOUR
When the soup is ready, season and serve.

CHUNKY CHICKEN SOUP

SERVES 4
chunky

| Calories: 280 | Protein: 30g | Fat: 5g | Carbs: 28g | Fibre: 6g |

Ingredients

- 1 medium leek, sliced
- 1 medium carrot, chopped
- 1 medium potato, chopped
- 100g frozen peas
- 1 celery stalk, sliced
- 1tsp dried thyme
- 1 garlic clove, sliced
- 600-800ml chicken stock
- 50g spinach, chopped
- 300g cooked chicken, shredded
- Salt & pepper for seasoning

Method

ONE
Add all the ingredients, except the spinach, chicken and seasoning, to your soup maker - making sure not to exceed the maximum fill line.

TWO
Combine all ingredients with a wooden spoon. Once done, place the lid on the soup maker and select the chunky setting.

THREE
Five minutes before the end of the cooking time pause the cycle and add the spinach and chicken. If your soup maker doesn't have a pause function just add at the end, stir and warm through.

FOUR
When the soup is ready, season and serve.

BEEF & APPLE SOUP

SERVES 4
● chunky

Calories: 365 | **Protein: 29g** | **Fat: 9g** | **Carbs: 38g** | **Fibre: 5g**

Ingredients

- 1 celery stalk, sliced
- 1 medium leek, sliced
- 1 medium onion, chopped
- 1 medium carrot, chopped
- 2 garlic cloves, sliced
- 2 tbsp tomato puree
- 400-600ml beef stock
- 200ml apple juice
- 300g cooked roast beef, chopped
- Salt & pepper for seasoning

Method

ONE
Add all the ingredients, except the beef and seasoning, to your soup maker - making sure not to exceed the maximum fill line.

TWO
Combine all ingredients with a wooden spoon. Once done, place the lid on the soup maker and select the chunky setting.

THREE
Five minutes before the end of the cooking time pause the cycle and add the beef. If your soup maker doesn't have a pause function just add at the end, stir and warm through.

FOUR
When the soup is ready, season and serve.

CHICKEN & FENNEL SOUP

SERVES 4
chunky

Calories: 380 | **Protein: 31g** | **Fat: 7g** | **Carbs: 45g** | **Fibre: 8g**

Ingredients

- 1 medium onion, chopped
- 2 medium carrots, chopped
- 150g pre-cooked pearl barley
- 1 garlic clove, sliced
- 1 tsp dried rosemary
- 600-800ml chicken stock
- 300g cooked chicken, shredded
- ¼ fennel bulb, very finely shredded
- Salt & pepper for seasoning

Method

ONE
Add all the ingredients, except the chicken, shredded fennel and seasoning, to your soup maker - making sure not to exceed the maximum fill line.

TWO
Combine all ingredients with a wooden spoon. Once done, place the lid on the soup maker and select the chunky setting.

THREE
Five minutes before the end of the cooking time pause the cycle and add the chicken. If your soup maker doesn't have a pause function just add at the end, stir and warm through.

FOUR
When the soup is ready, season and serve with shredded fennel sprinkled over the top of each bowl.

RUSTIC LAMB & VEGETABLE SOUP

SERVES 4
chunky

Calories: 250 | **Protein: 23g** | **Fat: 9g** | **Carbs: 15g** | **Fibre: 3g**

Ingredients

- 1 medium onion, chopped
- 1 medium carrot, chopped
- 1 celery stalk, sliced
- 1 tbsp tomato puree
- 1 garlic clove, sliced
- 1 tsp dried thyme
- 600ml-800ml chicken or lamb stock
- 200g cooked roast lamb, chopped
- Zest from 1 lemon
- Salt & pepper for seasoning

Method

ONE
Add all the ingredients, except the lamb, lemon zest and seasoning, to your soup maker - making sure not to exceed the maximum fill line.

TWO
Combine all ingredients with a wooden spoon. Once done, place the lid on the soup maker and select the chunky setting.

THREE
Five minutes before the end of the cooking time pause the cycle and add the lamb. If your soup maker doesn't have a pause function just add at the end, stir and warm through.

FOUR
When the soup is ready sprinkle with lemon zest, season and serve.

THAI CHICKEN SOUP

SERVES 4
⚙ chunky

Calories: 325 | **Protein: 35g** | **Fat: 6g** | **Carbs: 36g** | **Fibre: 6g**

Ingredients

- 1 medium carrot, chopped
- 1 medium onion, chopped
- 1 medium sweet potato, chopped
- 1 tbsp Thai red curry paste
- 600-800ml chicken stock
- 300g cooked chicken, shredded
- 150g packet straight-to-wok noodles, roughly chopped
- 2 tbsp soy sauce
- 100g beansprouts
- Salt & pepper for seasoning

Method

ONE
Add all the ingredients, except the chicken, noodles, soy sauce, beansprouts and seasoning, to your soup maker - making sure not to exceed the maximum fill line.

TWO
Combine all ingredients with a wooden spoon. Once done, place the lid on the soup maker and select the chunky setting.

THREE
Five minutes before the end of the cooking time pause the cycle to add the chicken and noodles. If your soup maker doesn't have a pause function just add at the end, stir and warm through.

FOUR
When the soup is ready, season and serve with soy sauce and beansprouts garnished over the top of each bowl.

BEEF & SPINACH SOUP

SERVES 4
chunky

Calories: 280 | Protein: 26g | Fat: 8g | Carbs: 22g | Fibre: 4g

Ingredients

- 1 medium onion, chopped
- 1 medium carrot, chopped
- 1 medium potato, chopped
- 1 tsp dried thyme
- 600ml-800ml beef stock
- 200g cooked roast beef,
- Zest of 1 lemon
- 25g spinach, finely chopped
- Salt & pepper for seasoning

Method

ONE
Add all the ingredients, except the beef, lemon zest, spinach and seasoning, to your soup maker - making sure not to exceed the maximum fill line.

TWO
Combine all ingredients with a wooden spoon. Once done, place the lid on the soup maker and select the chunky setting.

THREE
Five minutes before the end of the cooking time pause the cycle and add the beef. If your soup maker doesn't have a pause function just add at the end, stir and warm through.

FOUR
When the soup is ready, sprinkle the lemon zest and chopped spinach onto each bowl of soup. Season and serve.

CHICKEN & LEEK SOUP

SERVES 4
chunky

Calories: 250 | **Protein: 27g** | **Fat: 5g** | **Carbs: 24g** | **Fibre: 3g**

Ingredients

- 2 medium leeks, sliced
- 1 medium sweet potato, chopped
- 1 celery stalk, sliced
- 1 garlic clove, sliced
- 600-800ml chicken stock
- 300g cooked chicken, shredded
- 4 tbsp fresh chives, chopped
- Salt & pepper for seasoning

Method

ONE
Add all the ingredients, except the chicken, chives and seasoning, to your soup maker - making sure not to exceed the maximum fill line.

TWO
Combine all ingredients with a wooden spoon. Once done, place the lid on the soup maker and select the chunky setting.

THREE
Five minutes before the end of the cooking time pause the cycle and add the chicken. If your soup maker doesn't have a pause function just add at the end, stir and warm through.

FOUR
When the soup is ready, season and serve with chopped chives sprinkled over the top of each bowl.

ROSEMARY LAMB SOUP

SERVES 4
chunky

Calories: 280 | **Protein: 23g** | **Fat: 10g** | **Carbs: 21g** | **Fibre: 4g**

Ingredients

- 1 medium onion, chopped
- 1 medium potato, chopped
- 50g frozen peas
- 50g mushrooms, sliced
- 1 tbsp tomato puree
- 1 tbsp Worcestershire sauce
- 1 tbsp dried rosemary
- 600ml-800ml chicken or lamb stock
- 200g cooked roast lamb, chopped
- Salt & pepper for seasoning

Method

ONE
Add all the ingredients, except the lamb and seasoning, to your soup maker - making sure not to exceed the maximum fill line.

TWO
Combine all ingredients with a wooden spoon. Once done, place the lid on the soup maker and select the chunky setting.

THREE
Five minutes before the end of the cooking time pause the cycle and add the lamb. If your soup maker doesn't have a pause function just add at the end, stir and warm through.

FOUR
When the soup is ready, season and serve.

BEEF, TOMATO & RICE SOUP

SERVES 4
chunky

Calories: 360 | **Protein: 23g** | **Fat: 10g** | **Carbs: 43g** | **Fibre: 5g**

Ingredients

- 2 celery stalks, sliced
- 1 medium carrot, chopped
- 1 tin (400g) chopped tomatoes
- ½ pack (125g) pre-cooked white rice
- 200g cooked minced beef
- 2 garlic cloves, sliced
- 1 tsp paprika
- 400ml-600ml beef stock
- Salt & pepper for seasoning

Method

ONE
Add all the ingredients, except the seasoning, to your soup maker - making sure not to exceed the maximum fill line.

TWO
Combine all ingredients with a wooden spoon.

Three
Secure the lid on the soup maker and select the chunky setting.

FOUR
When the soup is ready, season and serve.

TURKEY & PUMPKIN SEED SOUP

SERVES 4
⚫ chunky

Calories: 270 | **Protein: 24g** | **Fat: 7g** | **Carbs: 27g** | **Fibre: 6g**

Ingredients

- 1 medium onion, chopped
- 1 medium carrot, chopped
- 1 celery stalk, sliced
- 1 tin (400g) chopped tomatoes
- 1 garlic clove, sliced
- 1 tsp dried thyme
- 400-600ml chicken stock
- 200g cooked turkey, shredded
- 2 tbsp pumpkin seeds, chopped
- Salt & pepper for seasoning

Method

ONE
Add all the ingredients, except the turkey, pumpkin seeds and seasoning to your soup maker - making sure not to exceed the maximum fill line.

TWO
Combine all ingredients with a wooden spoon. Once done, place the lid on the soup maker and select the chunky setting.

THREE
Five minutes before the end of the cooking time pause the cycle and add the turkey. If your soup maker doesn't have a pause function just add at the end, stir and warm through.

FOUR
When the soup is ready, season and serve with pumpkin seeds sprinkled over the top of each bowl.

CHICKEN SAUSAGE SOUP

SERVES 4
chunky

Calories: 280 | **Protein: 23g** | **Fat: 12g** | **Carbs: 17g** | **Fibre: 3g**

Ingredients

- 1 medium onion, chopped
- 1 medium carrot, chopped
- 1 garlic clove, sliced
- 1 tsp dried thyme
- 600ml-800ml chicken stock
- 4 pre-cooked chicken sausages, diced
- 50g spinach, chopped
- Salt & pepper for seasoning

Method

ONE
Add all the ingredients, except the sausages, spinach and seasoning to your soup maker - making sure not to exceed the maximum fill line.

TWO
Combine all ingredients with a wooden spoon. Once done, place the lid on the soup maker and select the chunky setting.

THREE
Five minutes before the end of the cooking time pause the cycle to add the sausages and spinach. If your soup maker doesn't have a pause function just add at the end, stir and warm through.

FOUR
When the soup is ready season and serve.

NUTTY BEEF SOUP

SERVES 4
⊙ chunky

Calories: 390 | **Protein: 28g** | **Fat: 16g** | **Carbs: 29g** | **Fibre: 6g**

Ingredients

- 1 medium onion, chopped
- 1 celery stalk, sliced
- 1 tin (400g) chopped tomatoes
- 300g cooked minced beef
- 2 garlic cloves, sliced
- 1 tsp dried thyme
- 400-500ml beef stock
- 2 tbsp almonds, chopped
- 2 tbsp fresh flat leaf parsley, chopped
- Salt & pepper for seasoning

Method

ONE
Add all the ingredients, except the almonds, parsley and seasoning, to your soup maker - making sure not to exceed the maximum fill line.

TWO
Combine all ingredients with a wooden spoon.

THREE
Secure the lid on the soup maker and select the chunky setting.

FOUR
When the soup is ready sprinkle over the almonds and parsley. Season and serve.

SPICED LAMB BOWL

SERVES 4
chunky

Calories: 330 | Protein: 23g | Fat: 6g | Carbs: 42g | Fibre: 14g

Ingredients

- 1 medium onion, chopped
- 1 celery stalk, sliced
- ½ tin (200g) chopped tomatoes
- 1 tin (390g) cooked lentils, rinsed
- 1 garlic clove, sliced
- ½ tsp ground cumin
- ½ tsp ground coriander
- 1 tsp paprika
- 300ml-500ml chicken or lamb stock
- 100g cooked roast lamb, chopped
- Salt & pepper for seasoning

Method

ONE
Add all the ingredients, except the lamb and seasoning, to your soup maker - making sure not to exceed the maximum fill line.

TWO
Combine all ingredients with a wooden spoon. Once done, place the lid on the soup maker and select the chunky setting.

THREE
Five minutes before the end of the cooking time pause the cycle and add the lamb. If your soup maker doesn't have a pause function just add at the end, stir and warm through.

FOUR
When the soup is ready, season and serve.

TURKEY & COURGETTE SOUP

SERVES 4
chunky

Calories: 210 | **Protein: 22g** | **Fat: 2g** | **Carbs: 27g** | **Fibre: 6g**

Ingredients

- 1 medium onion, chopped
- 1 medium carrot, chopped
- 1 celery stalk, sliced
- 1 tin (400g) chopped tomatoes
- 2 medium courgettes
- 1 garlic clove, sliced
- 1 tsp dried oregano
- 400-600ml chicken stock
- 200g cooked turkey, shredded
- Salt & pepper for seasoning

Method

ONE
Dice one of the courgettes. With the other, use a vegetable peeler to create delicate flesh ribbons and set these ribbons aside.

TWO
Add all the ingredients, except the turkey, courgette ribbons and seasoning to your soup maker - making sure not to exceed the maximum fill line. Combine all ingredients with a wooden spoon. Once done, place the lid on the soup maker and select the chunky setting.

THREE
Five minutes before the end of the cooking time pause the cycle and add the turkey. If your soup maker doesn't have a pause function just add at the end, stir and warm through.

FOUR
When the soup is ready, season and serve with the courgette ribbons piled on top of each bowl of soup.

CAULIFLOWER-TOPPED BEEF SOUP

SERVES 4
chunky

Calories: 280 | **Protein: 24g** | **Fat: 8g** | **Carbs: 25g** | **Fibre: 6g**

Ingredients

- 2 celery stalks, sliced
- 1 medium carrot, chopped
- 1 tin (400g) chopped tomatoes
- 2 garlic cloves, sliced
- 1 tsp dried thyme
- 400ml-600ml beef stock
- 200g cooked roast beef, chopped
- ¼ cauliflower head, grated
- Salt & pepper for seasoning

Method

ONE
Add all the ingredients, except the beef, cauliflower and seasoning, to your soup maker - making sure not to exceed the maximum fill line.

TWO
Combine all ingredients with a wooden spoon. Once done, place the lid on the soup maker and select the chunky setting.

THREE
Five minutes before the end of the cooking time pause the cycle to add the beef. If your soup maker doesn't have a pause function just add at the end, stir and warm through.

Four
When the soup is ready sprinkle over the grated cauliflower. Season with lots of black pepper and serve.

LAMB & SPINACH SOUP

SERVES 4
⊛ chunky

Calories: 320 | Protein: 27g | Fat: 13g | Carbs: 22g | Fibre: 5g

Ingredients

- 1 medium onion, chopped
- 1 medium carrot, chopped
- 1 medium potato, chopped
- 1 garlic clove, sliced
- 600ml-800ml beef or lamb stock
- 200g cooked roast lamb, chopped
- 50g spinach, chopped
- 2 tbsp fresh flat leaf parsley, chopped
- Salt & pepper for seasoning

Method

ONE
Add all the ingredients, except the lamb, spinach, parsley and seasoning, to your soup maker - making sure not to exceed the maximum fill line.

TWO
Combine all ingredients with a wooden spoon. Once done, place the lid on the soup maker and select the chunky setting.

THREE
Five minutes before the end of the cooking time pause the cycle to add the lamb and spinach. If your soup maker doesn't have a pause function just add at the end, stir and warm through.

FOUR
When the soup is ready sprinkle with parsley, season and serve.

ITALIAN BEEF SOUP

Calories: 244 | **Protein: 19g** | **Fat: 12g** | **Carbs: 16g** | **Fibre:4g**

Ingredients

- 1 medium onion, chopped
- 1 medium sweet potato, chopped
- 1 tin (400g) chopped tomatoes
- 2 tbsp tomato puree
- 2 garlic cloves, sliced
- 1 bunch fresh basil, chopped
- 300g cooked minced beef
- 400-500ml beef stock
- Salt & pepper for seasoning

Method

ONE
Add all the ingredients, except the seasoning, to your soup maker - making sure not to exceed the maximum fill line.

TWO
Combine all ingredients with a wooden spoon.

THREE
Secure the lid on the soup maker and select the chunky setting.

FOUR
When the soup is ready, season and serve.

SIMPLE FISH SOUP

Calories: 180 | **Protein: 22g** | **Fat: 2g** | **Carbs: 16g** | **Fibre: 4g**

Ingredients

- 2 medium onions, chopped
- 1 red pepper, sliced
- 1 tin (400g) chopped tomatoes
- 2 tbsp tomato puree
- 2 garlic cloves, sliced
- 1 tsp dried thyme
- 1 tsp dried oregano
- 1 tsp paprika
- 400ml-600ml vegetable or fish stock
- 200g cooked white fish fillets
- 2 tbsp fresh parsley, chopped
- Salt & pepper for seasoning

Method

ONE
Add all the ingredients, except the fish, parsley and seasoning, to your soup maker - making sure not to exceed the maximum fill line.

TWO
Combine all ingredients with a wooden spoon. Once done, place the lid on the soup maker and select the chunky setting.

THREE
Five minutes before the end of the cooking time pause the cycle and add the fish. If your soup maker doesn't have a pause function just add at the end, stir and warm through.

FOUR
When the soup is ready sprinkle with parsley. Season and serve.

FISH & COCONUT SOUP

SERVES 4
chunky

Calories: 260 | **Protein: 21g** | **Fat: 10g** | **Carbs: 21g** | **Fibre: 4g**

Ingredients

- 1 medium onion, chopped
- 2 red or yellow peppers, sliced
- 1 tin (400g) chopped tomatoes
- 2 garlic cloves, sliced
- I tbsp Thai red curry paste
- 2 tbsp tomato puree
- 300ml-500ml vegetable or fish stock
- 100ml low-fat coconut milk
- 200g cooked white fish fillets
- Zest of 1 lime
- Salt & pepper for seasoning

Method

ONE
Add all the ingredients, except the fish, lime zest and seasoning, to your soup maker - making sure not to exceed the maximum fill line.

TWO
Combine all ingredients with a wooden spoon. Once done, place the lid on the soup maker and select the chunky setting.

THREE
Five minutes before the end of the cooking time pause the cycle and add the fish. If your soup maker doesn't have a pause function just add at the end, stir and warm through.

FOUR
When the soup is ready sprinkle with lime zest. Season and serve.

HADDOCK & EGG SOUP

SERVES 4
chunky

Calories: 280 | **Protein: 27g** | **Fat: 9g** | **Carbs: 24g** | **Fibre: 4g**

Ingredients

- 1 medium onion, chopped
- 2 medium carrots, chopped
- 1 garlic clove, sliced
- 500ml-700ml vegetable or fish stock
- 200ml semi-skimmed milk
- 200g cooked white fish fillets
- 4 hardboiled eggs, chopped
- Salt & pepper for seasoning

Method

ONE
Add all the ingredients, except the milk, fish, eggs and seasoning, to your soup maker - making sure not to exceed the maximum fill line.

TWO
Combine all ingredients with a wooden spoon. Once done, place the lid on the soup maker and select the chunky setting.

THREE
Five minutes before the end of the cooking time pause the cycle and add the milk and fish. If your soup maker doesn't have a pause function just add at the end, stir and warm through.

FOUR
When the soup is ready top the soup with chopped eggs. Season and serve.

LEEK & HADDOCK SOUP

SERVES 4
chunky

Calories: 320 | **Protein: 24g** | **Fat: 9g** | **Carbs: 35g** | **Fibre: 5g**

Ingredients

- 2 medium leeks, sliced
- 2 medium potatoes, chopped
- 1 garlic clove, sliced
- 1 tsp dried thyme
- 400ml-600ml vegetable or fish stock
- 200ml semi-skimmed milk
- 200g cooked white fish fillets
- 2 celery stalks, finely chopped
- Salt & pepper for seasoning

Method

ONE
Add all the ingredients, except the milk, fish, celery and seasoning, to your soup maker - making sure not to exceed the maximum fill line.

TWO
Combine all ingredients with a wooden spoon. Once done, place the lid on the soup maker and select the chunky setting.

THREE
Five minutes before the end of the cooking time pause the cycle and add the milk and fish. If your soup maker doesn't have a pause function just add at the end, stir and warm through.

FOUR
When the soup is ready top the soup with the finely chopped celery. Season and serve.

CURRIED SALMON SOUP

SERVES 4
chunky

Calories: 320 | **Protein: 25g** | **Fat: 12g** | **Carbs: 29g** | **Fibre: 5g**

Ingredients

- 1 medium onion, chopped
- 1 medium potato, chopped
- 1 medium carrot, chopped
- 1 garlic clove, sliced
- 1 tbsp medium curry powder
- 400ml-600ml vegetable or fish stock
- 200ml low-fat coconut milk
- 200g cooked salmon fillets
- 2 tbsp fresh coriander, chopped
- Salt & pepper for seasoning

Method

ONE
Add all the ingredients, except the coconut milk, fish, coriander and seasoning, to your soup maker - making sure not to exceed the maximum fill line.

TWO
Combine all ingredients with a wooden spoon. Once done, place the lid on the soup maker and select the chunky setting.

THREE
Five minutes before the end of the cooking time pause the cycle and add the coconut milk and fish. If your soup maker doesn't have a pause function just add at the end, stir and warm through.

FOUR
When the soup is ready top with chopped coriander. Season and serve.

VEGETABLE STOCK

Ingredients

- 1 tbsp olive oil
- 1 medium onion, chopped
- 2 medium carrots, chopped
- 1 medium leek, sliced
- 2 celery stalks, sliced
- 3 garlic cloves, sliced
- 1 tsp thyme
- 1 tbsp black peppercorns
- 2 bay leaves
- 1 tsp salt
- 3 litres water

Method

ONE
Heat the olive oil in a saucepan and gently sauté the onions, carrots, leeks, celery, garlic and thyme for a few minutes.

TWO
Add the remaining ingredients and bring to the boil. Leave to gently simmer for 30 minutes with a lid on.

THREE
Allow to cool for a little while. Pour the stock into a bowl through a sieve to separate the solid ingredients. Discard the contents of the sieve.

FOUR
Store the stock in the fridge for a day or two or freeze in batches.

CHICKEN STOCK

Ingredients

- 1 tbsp olive oil
- 2 medium onions, chopped
- 2 medium carrots, chopped
- 2 celery stalks, sliced
- 1 leftover roast chicken carcass
- 2 bay leaves
- 1 tsp dried thyme
- 1 tsp salt
- 1 tsp black peppercorns
- 3 litres water

Method

ONE
Heat the olive oil in a saucepan and gently sauté the onions, carrots and celery for a few minutes.

TWO
Add the remaining ingredients and bring to the boil. Leave to gently simmer for 30 minutes with the lid on.

THREE
Allow to cool for a little while. Pour the stock into a bowl through a sieve to separate the solid ingredients. Discard the contents of the sieve.

FOUR
Store the stock in the fridge for a day or two or freeze in batches.

FISH STOCK

Ingredients

- 1 tbsp olive oil
- 2 medium onions, chopped
- 3 medium carrots, chopped
- 1 celery stalk, sliced
- 1 leek, sliced
- 1 tbsp black peppercorns
- 1 tsp dried thyme
- 500g fish bones, heads, carcasses etc
- 1 tsp salt
- 3 litres water

Method

ONE
Heat the olive oil in a saucepan and gently sauté the onions, carrots, celery and leeks for a few minutes.

TWO
Add the remaining ingredients and bring to the boil. Leave to gently simmer for 30 minutes with the lid on.

THREE
Allow to cool for a little while. Pour the stock into a bowl through a sieve to separate the solid ingredients. Discard the contents of the sieve.

FOUR
Store the stock in the fridge for a day or two or freeze in batches.

BEEF STOCK

Ingredients

- 1 tbsp olive oil
- 2 medium onions, chopped
- 2 medium carrots, chopped
- 2 celery stalks, sliced
- 3 garlic cloves, sliced
- 1 tbsp black peppercorns
- 2 bay leaves
- 1 tsp dried thyme
- 1kg beef bones
- 1 tsp salt
- 3 litres water

Method

ONE
Heat the olive oil in a saucepan and gently sauté the onions, carrots, celery and garlic for a few minutes.

TWO
Add the remaining ingredients and bring to the boil. Leave to gently simmer for 30 minutes with the lid on.

THREE
Allow to cool for a little while. Pour the stock into a bowl through a sieve to separate the solid ingredients. Discard the contents of the sieve.

FOUR
Store the stock in the fridge for a day or two or freeze in batches.

Printed in Great Britain
by Amazon